All Appears Ordinary
Freya Bantiff

the poetry business

Published 2024 by
New Poets List
The Poetry Business
Campo House,
54 Campo Lane,
Sheffield S1 2EG

Copyright © Freya Bantiff 2024
All Rights Reserved

ISBN 978-1-914914-74-4
eBook ISBN 978-1-914914-75-1
Typeset by Utter

Designed and typeset by Utter
Printed by Biddles Books

Smith|Doorstop Books are a member of Inpress:
www.inpressbooks.co.uk

Distributed by NBN International, 1 Deltic Avenue,
Rooksley, Milton Keynes MK13 8LD

The Poetry Business gratefully acknowledges
the support of Arts Council England.

Contents

5	Mum Sends Me an Article on Death Cleaning
6	Other People's Lives
7	God the Whale
8	'Our Little Brown Rat'
10	Dinner Invitation
11	The Lie of the Land
12	The Photographer
13	I Want to Walk Where the Whelks Washed Up
14	The Removal Process
15	Grandpa's Sky Lantern
16	Yes
17	What Schrödinger's Cat and My Bisexuality Have in Common
18	I Hope This Email Finds You
20	I Wish I Could Google Facts About My Friends
21	Flight of the Optimist
22	After the Bleaching
24	If Someone Told Me on a Date That They Liked the Idea of Human Composting
25	Reasons Not to Visit the Rijksmuseum with the Wrong Person
26	As the Platypus Does
27	Failed Resurrection
28	The Lord God Bird
29	Working Debenhams' Late Shift
32	Acknowledgements

For my parents, who have always been supportive, and especially my mum, who has read every poem along the way.

Mum Sends Me an Article on Death Cleaning

Do you want me to do it, she asks, 87% joking,
indicating the instructions to *evaluate abundance, remove
an element of emotional burden, ask 'will someone
be happier if I keep this?'* As if after 50, identity
is just breathing's paraphernalia. *Fuck no,* I say.
Most unmeditative, but back when I practised yoga,
they taught us that attachment causes *suffering,*
that objects and people create heavyweight
wanting, that we must cultivate *healthy separation* like a hand
held binbag slack. A pre-mourned present, black
and billowing. On the mat, I placed my palms
onto a stranger's sweaty handprint stains, felt phantom
pulse as I contorted into a cat, a dog, a lizard,
trying to see why the suffering wasn't worth it. *Let go
with the breath,* the instructor said. I still have
every letter from every blotted lover I've ever had,
hope to leave a small scandal in a box of pages,
pressed as white flags, surrendered, tissues
carefully unscrunched. I still keep a worry stone
conker on my desk from that season I loaded my pockets
with them, trying not to sink, along with headphones
that work best when tangled, a half-used
candle from the half-burnt ambitions of three new years'
past, so when I'm old, don't ask me to pack
myself into a cardboard box waiting room. Not while
the pot fern might grow better now the brown
is cut back and my notes app is working on a hair knot
of loose threads. Let me stay in this odds and ends, bits
and bobs, sewing box, biscuit tin, past its sell-by date
joy. Let me love this existence a little while longer.

Other People's Lives

Passing that house trekking home I'm not sure
if they're taking down the wall or rebuilding it, but
I could rhapsodise about weak points in hedges,
become a midge-ball of restless wonder by every gate
just swinging open. Cars are happening somewhere

and the foxglove's furry stem looks scalable
as if I also could rest on a lean-to like a shoulder. From there
every roof-sheltered place is a skin. Slip me into it:
I'll call, *honey I'm back*, just to see if anyone answers
and try to translate *lucy on wed @ 6, dan from finance*.

I'll open the fridge and consume goods long-expired.
I might use the best cutlery. I might study how
their spoon fits in my mouth, how their clothes hang
from my shoulders. By the bed,
I'll find someone's water and sip on it, then in a spritz

I'll discover if I am patchouli, tonka, lavender –
and perhaps I'll bin all my makeup or hook
bondage chains from my ceiling or afford skiing
every winter and it's all downhill
from here. What if I now like a pint? What if I don't keep

the porch light switched on for strangers
navigating streets? The moon gleams
on the window ledge like another life I dropped
and need to pick up and I feel so close to it, its face
is my face, though neither of us understands the other.

God the Whale

Sometimes I imagine the sun striking midday will drop
in a hand's motion and smite me. Confess your crime:
mine is to love like the craftsman's apprentice
who never dirties her hands in acting. My dad's is arguing.
In the debate about the divine watchmaker, he lists
mutating viruses, parasitic worms, the test runs
of extinction and I say if God exists, I think they might
be a whale. Unfathomed and wildering. No cogs
and quick fingers. Just this warm blooded, blubbered God
on a migration path I can't follow. Perhaps this is because
if God sang a song, I am certain it would cover

vast distances. It would be peaceful

as weeping and if whales could cry, God would.
They say God saw the world and it was *good* but this is
omniscience tangled in ghost gear, surfacing
through oil slicks, starving for sustenance in a sea
brought to simmer. We barrel into God at 25 knots
and God swallows it – our loneliness and toothbrushes,
bitterness and broken sandals, so when we send up
plankton bloom prayers God has no room
to stomach them, becomes deaf to all but military sonar,
seismic surveys and this: the waterlogged clock,
the leaking battery, the alarm ringing in God's gut.

'Our Little Brown Rat'

> Title quote comes from Tim Beshara, The
> Wilderness Society. The Bramble Cay melomys
> was the first mammal to be declared extinct as a
> result of the climate crisis/rising sea levels.

We return for you like a storm
surge or visiting birds –
a disturbance, but we try to land
lightly. It is late in the year.

You are here: citation needed.
The string of your tail should have
had a knot so we couldn't forget.
Prehensile and mosaic-patterned:

you see the value of broken
pieces – arrived on driftwood
or a vanished land bridge
so you must know connections

can't be trusted. No one said it,
but you were too ugly
for publicity. Matted and coarse,
last time, we found the fallen

chestnut of you, soaked, as though
before roasting. Even your whiskers
shivered, as if there was a breeze
we couldn't feel. The chill

comes in a blink as we scour
the cay for nest sites, scat,
crackle of you in vegetation,
scuffle of you in sand – appoint

cameras like lifeguards,
set hair-trigger traps only
to watch them fill with salt.
You are the first of the everyday

lost, exquisite
in it. We toast with flasks
to your name as the tide
inches up towards our feet.

Dinner Invitation

She can't forget the fireflies
though the man in front of her
is blindingly attractive and has booked
a candlelit restaurant where they toast
with cut glass *to desire*. She wants
to tell him but he wouldn't want to hear

how the males burst up
from the grasses as she headed out,
burning their tick mark flights in an airborne rush
of *yes yes yes* and she'd lingered
too long, her sandalled feet sinking
into the moss. And then there were some

it had taken her longer to figure out –
fireflies like stars changing constellations,
lighthouses lying, who would imitate
the mating flashes of other species
and eat the suitors. When she caught one,
legs and wings protruded from its mouth.

It's females that do this,
she tells herself. She lets him
walk her home, lets him pull her
towards him like a chemical
to its reaction – the double lens of his glasses
flaring up under the streetlamps.

The Lie of the Land

Though it should not be accepted from a lover
in bed, naked, limbs criss-crossed in promises,
I try to take it as a compliment when
the sonographer tells me, *you have exceptionally
ordinary breasts*, as she smears the jelly out over
the tiny peaks. Eyes still studying
the screen. I tell her, *I am from Sheffield*, find

myself speaking about home, the seven hills
and five rivers as she tries to locate something
I cannot name but might be inside of me – and I
am recalling that time I almost died, descending
Mam Tor in the black shale night, tripping

the gradient of a nightmare. I know how
to look at these breasts as if they belong
someplace else. *Here*, she says, *you may feel
a little pressure*, then she asks me about

my mother's cancer, which grew in grapes,
not one but as a cluster, underripe, yet everything
burst at once. The leaflet said, *do tell them
if it is uncomfortable*, but she is removing
the transducer from my skin, leaving me sticky,

explaining how the probe collects sounds
that bounce back and the images can even show
blood flowing through vessels and, *yes, all appears
ordinary*, as I slide off the table – gleeful
as water running off a slope to its river, looking
down now at the lumps of flesh on my chest,
which are, after all, just parts of my body.

The Photographer

He's not interested in the rich pendants of sweat hanging
from the glassmaker's brow – only the heat of the day
which is blown, becoming an object, glossy

and desirable. This, amongst many things, is new to me.
It seems Venice has a market, stinking ammonia like a dying
sea. It appears he'd choose a restaurant frontage

over a cat. *It's more precious,* he declares, *to take
a photo in analogue,* so when he shifts his camera away
from ordered capstones, archways, canals and onto me, I try

to feel flattered. Does it matter if I am just another
unknown place that he's visiting? My spine, a stone
bridge bending backwards to his touch. My height, a balcony

for him to peer at himself.

I Want to Walk Where the Whelks Washed Up

Sunnyside beach, Devon. Spilled sugar beach, sand
still dark and eye gunk gritty. I blink, and it stays
beautiful. I am seven again and wear age like a light jacket
I'll grow into. Windblown, I outrun myself. I rewind
myself. Everyone is healthy. We have packed sandwiches
in foil, nacre-sheened, which means a day out, which means
precious, mother of pearl. It is so early, I think that no one
has ever walked here, that we are the first odd fish
to leave the ocean, inelegant, flopping upwards
in waterproof clothing. And they are strewn everywhere.
The whelks. The first one, large as the French
cricket ball my dad teaches me to catch, the second fat
as my Samsung flip phone. I am appetite, greedy hands
grasping, glugging belly laughter. They are so many;
I have so much to hold onto. Water wells up in their empty
chambers and no one cries. I shake one and water
overflows. Each shell is a spiral, a narrowing, a one-way
road. I am seven. I have not made any decisions. I sit
at the widest part of the beach and stare out as the calm
comes in, heavy as overwalked legs. I could dive down.
I could paint pictures. I could be a good person. I hold
one whelk up to my ear, hear openness. I keep listening.

The Removal Process

You may remember the nits
and the fine-toothed comb your mother used
to part your hair without drag
as she drew it down from crown to ends.

A cotton towel draped around your shoulders.
Your childhood pillow soaked in boiling water.
The repetitive pull like a pulse in the bloodstream
of *I'm here I'm here I'm here*

before she slicked your head with shampoo
and conditioner, ached your neck back
over the sink where the lather pooled
and sucked. Nothing caught but this truth:

she never wished you to carry more
than you had to. So, she'd pick out every bead
of casing and bloated adult, replace them
with hands that slid off the strands

as leaves fall away at the season's close –
the air left a little altered.

Grandpa's Sky Lantern

He held

the lantern out in an invite to air, where it billowed
like a single paper pantaloon – Sheffield's last

crucible reheated, molten strength straining towards
a stainless sky, stars patterning a dizziness

of dots over iris, the night weighed down with light
already. Why were we sending more

up there? I don't know, but I was an oxygen
child, consumed with wick of wonder – not yet

worried about whether a farmer would find
his field burning with poker barley, if a fox would snare

its foot on the wire frame once the light limped out, if
out at sea, the lantern would look too jellyfish

and a leatherback would bite down. I only
stood, as my grandpa let it loose, with a glow

inside me, burning blood, my mouth so
wide with laughter, I could have swallowed it whole.

Yes

we were at the graveyard, in a smug little village, sixth
form school trip, meant to be learning Latin, ancient
Greek, and you wanted to go home, *domus,* but I wasn't
ready to bury you   and yes I suggested Kate Bush,
scared of spending forever speaking dead languages
to you, then stared while you sang along, notes ghosting
your lips   and yes I was dancing on the stone slabs,
badly, a twist-legged tornado hurtling towards you, tripping
truth impact, just to get you to look at me   and yes
there was the church, its crypt below with all those candles
burning under our feet, where tomorrow you would
light one and I would push you against a pillar, kiss
as you only can when young, hands not large enough
to grasp all you want, pupils hubris dilated, but I
didn't know that yet   and yes it was disrespectful
and yes a priest heard his graveyard bone-laughing,
shouting, and ran at us, mouth running ahead   and yes
out on the wily windy moors we'd roll and fall in green
and yes the grit in my knees took an age to wash
out, like *domain* rinsed from *domus*   and yes I lived
in the wounds, too ashamed to be seen, wore leggings
all week in the sun while they wept and stuck   and yes
I said sorry, though I knew I wouldn't have minded, if I
were dead, and lovers danced all over me, all that breath
coming fast, heels pounding heat, rousing me, raising
me – what wouldn't I have done to be touched.

What Schrödinger's Cat and My Bisexuality Have in Common

A dry amusement at attempts to verify
their reality. An existence that persists
when unobserved. A sensual strut
that borders on slink. A tendency to walk
both feet first. Wakefulness at dusk.
Retractable claws. Recoil response
from strangers' hands. Ability to curl
into a question mark and not be seen.
Uncertainty as to whether trying to come
out would be a death or liberation.
Worlds that are full of reactivity.
Inane questions. Jokes where the punchline
is *pussy*. A suspicion carried
by the scruff of the neck that many
lives will be lived, but never all
recognised. Inner purr of conviction.
Fear of having no room to stretch
out. An innate loathing of boxes.

I Hope This Email Finds You

off-grid, anti-cubicle, tramping some unchartered
transect with real mice, nothing stationary, remote
without the work, threading thoughts
as loose as daisies, hooked through the quiet
spaces. Tell me that you are discovering
the millstone grit of legs, muscles contracting
like cut-off pleasantries, no *please,* no *kind regards* –
just squeeze of own ambition gaining height
as you cover spread sheet moors, always more
and more, creaseless, ceaseless, scribbled
in lengthy skylines. What if you disappeared

here – where the grouse used to dart from dot-to-dot
bullets, until stapled down – here, where obligations
slow like flies in sundew, stuck, the day digesting,
heather gentling with bruises. You could
stop, if you wanted. You could rest, lying
in wavy hair-grass, with ants and soldier
beetles and frogs, heart starting
to leap, before taking a crack at the rocks
with your heels, racing where giants ran,
setting the pace, in this place where Merlin hawks
cast spells in seconds, all eyes

spiralling up, magic springy underfoot, ever
for the outside, the outsiders. Even stones
speak, scratch fylfots, grooves and cups. You could drink
it all up. Rise refreshed, fist-first, full-throttled,

boxing from bracken and bramble, a slam
to the slog, decking the drudgery. Look at you
striking out, hot-blooded, life-lithe, alive, more
than March mad, under kestrel
email circling and thinking better of it, finding you
a hair too fast, a hare too strong, too much
a part of this place.

I Wish I Could Google Facts About My Friends

Such as, *title of favourite podcast.* I remember
it featured jackets (?) or raincoats (?) and was narrated
by a mouse. You talked about it on Saturday
while winding pasta, messily, each strand squiggling
some meaning of existence. I unravel. *What is the date
of your next interview? Which side has the dead
grandparents? Who are you?* Asking is too close

to admission of emptiness, binary code blipping
an error message, browser stuck on blue screen. I've tried,
in the past, to form a fact file for each person. Crime
scene style. After each meeting, I'd add to it, punching
keys to beat the rush to forgetting. *Brother called
Jeremy, owns one tabby cat archetype, going
on holiday to Switzerland (?) – began with 's'.*

Even as a kid, my Nintendo DS Secret Diary asked me
to enter my people, design their profiles. Hair. Freckles.
I was better at appearances. My librarian friend
tells me that looks can be deceiving, so things
must be referenced in systems, indexes, Dewey –
dew like a morning, everything colour-coded,
crystallised. And when I date a museum curator

who agonises over storage boxes, he asks me what
I'd save. *Books,* I think. *Plants. Instruments.* Settle on
details. It would be nice to hold people
that carefully. To trust that everything was stored
in the right conditions. To know how to keep them.

Flight of the Optimist

Not one of those men who'd relish
how the birds sang warnings
at his approach but that evening,
to impress me, he called me out
to the balcony over the forest, which trembled
as an afterlife, on the brink
of full night, and he pulled up an app
which he used to trick the owl
with her mating call. One hand tapped
play, play – the other clutched the dead
wood of my arm. I itched
to stretch it. He didn't notice
that I was shivering – only the inhuman
noise pulled from me like that shape
from the shadows as she came with the slow
drag of possibility and cool air brushing
the fringe of her feathers. Light
as an eyelash blown for luck, unruffled
as a cloud swept off course
and it was not wisdom, just
necessity, that saw me following her path
as she swooped in, over
and over, hopelessly circling
above him, searching for something
that wasn't there.

After the Bleaching

> *By 2050, 90% of global coral reefs are projected to experience coral bleaching annually*
> – Coral Reef Alliance.

If he can capture the coral's spawn
slicks in this net like dreams

in a catcher, raise them, over months,
into reality and release them,

perhaps hope has a reason
to be out, so round and full tonight.

He thinks he might be content if only
they can keep all the colour

of the earth right here – a younger
memory suspended in ocean,

like strawberries in syrup, glitter
in a globe, as they lose the rest –

to those things that trouble
the surface but rarely break it. At least,

until now. When that happens,
he might cry but he will not sink

into it. He will dive down, deeper and
deeper. His feet will settle

on the seabed, softly, supported
by these offspring of survivors.

The pressure will be crushing
yet he knows he will breathe so easily.

If Someone Told Me on a Date That They Liked the Idea of Human Composting

I think I might fall in love.

I want to go the same way
as banana skins and potato peel. I want to be a bed
of wood chips, alfalfa and heat-loving
thermophilic microbes. I want to tell you the forecast
as a pine cone. I want to be a rose bush. I want to be
your oxygen.

Imagine such a lover. Who would fuck
like a life cycle, born and dying, born
and dying, messy and mucosal. Who would want
your undomesticated wilderness, full handfuls
of your hips. Who wouldn't be afraid
to break down, to turn DNA into divinity.
Who, instead of fast cars and flash clothes, would give you
a single thimble of topsoil, teeming
with tiny organisms.

If you lost a lover like that, it would be a tree
falling where no one hears it but the whole ground
shakes. You would need to take rubbings
of their fingerprints to remember how it felt
to be embraced by the romance of a canopy.

This would be the lover who would lay down
their body to make new paths, leave their footprints
all over you without weight, say they've seen God
while gardening, then offer you flowers from their eyes,
know how to give back all that they took.

Reasons Not to Visit the Rijksmuseum with the Wrong Person

Catching the eye of a Greek statue, I know it. Paris
is baby boyish, dummy apple clutched tight
as choice, and I hate him a little – aware that in another
room, I have left the man I brought here finding
himself amongst the flintlock pistols, wheellock
rifles, matchlock muskets, and anything
that has a fatal trigger. I have tried
talk. It has passed in bullet hole full stop, blown up
in the great between-us, and now there are deader
things than autopsy or mummy. There is
a stuffed hand leaking through skin bandages. I don't
try to touch it. Art holds feeling and this
doesn't. Even the protective lighting, halo dimmed,
won't hide it. There is damage occurring in disinterest,
so I distract with the etching of a doctor, made
from lines incised into metal using acid, as if healing
requires hurt. The man I brought is still
looking at weaponry while I walk to the gallery's
end, where there is a saint's head on a platter. Salome,
eyes averted. Salome, carrying the weight
of blood loss. Salome, smiling beyond the frame,
unafraid to cause pain, because she danced so nicely,
and the king promised her *anything*. And the king
asked her, *what do you want? What do you
want?* and I know the answer. Her hips swing, bellish,
as I exit the hall, so aware of my footsteps.

As the Platypus Does

I am going to love myself – all the ungainly
bits   untutored   stuck at unfeasible
angles   where knowledgeable men scratch
their heads   try to spot the stitches – *how
does she do it –   what holds her
together?* This toothless torpedo-shaped
body warzone   unsolved riddle
of creature   unpopped balloon
buoyancy with bone dense ballast. I like
their grandma's-accessories-all-worn-
at-once chic   their off-piste anti-establishment
unsuitedness   their wing and a prayer
weirdness   sifting insects shellfish
small shrimp from substrate and finding
sweetness. It must be nice. To sleep often
and deeply   slipping under attention's
surface   just serenity streamlined
with no need to hibernate   to find
yourself waterproof   everything running
off   a thick layer of air trapped
everywhere   to close eyes ears nostrils
become pure feeling   electroreceptors
tingling touch   like good thoughts caught
midstream   to live digging and swimming
full-bellied juxtaposition. Semi-aquatic
semi-accepted   wholly self – a brain splashing
joyfully with rubber duck absurdity
in a bathtub   saying *take from this river-life
this world-box   everything that you think fits.*

Failed Resurrection

It might seem ignominious, how we held
the funeral. Each school assembly,

we butchered *All Things Bright and Beautiful*,
while Jesus died and rose, shawled
in sermons, like a party trick,
but the bee stayed dead. We poked it

where it lay, just out, past the touchline.
We made dandelion offerings, while the bee
stayed still, furry, as if pollen-fuzzed
by sleep. Our hands scooped it
up, carried this feeling of unfairness
until we found a Sunny Raisin snack box
coffin – lined it with grass (for comfort), a nettle
(for sting) and a bindweed petal, ghost-pale,
pinched from the wall that bordered
the graveyard. My atheist friend recited
The Lord's Prayer. I tucked the bee in

like a dawn into darkness – insisting
that it mattered. Then we lobbed that tiny,
golden, buzz-less wish into idol flight, up
and over the wall, like a brick thrown

through a window, in the planet's
smallest protest.

The Lord God Bird

As of May 2024, debate continues regarding the Lord God Bird's survival or extinction

He exists now as a hole pecked through the centre
of the universe where debate expands. Confirmed reports say
since His paradise fell, He has been shot, frequently,

sometimes eaten, and was tender, though the bones
could catch in the throat. Remains have been identified,
or relics, and as He could do anything – consume

poison ivy seeds – appear after sixty years above Cache River –
there are believers. Pilgrims trekking through hardwood
and coniferous, who hear the double knock and see

doors opened for them in grainy photos or in a single
secondary feather rescued from the roost of a storm-split
tree. They search for where His bill has peeled back

bark to reveal the hidden paths but hardly anyone
has seen Him. Those who claim to speak of the burning
crest that crowned Him, discoid halo of each gold-piece eye.

Easier to talk, than to conjure the awe and love slashed
white across His wings as He rises like a meteor,
burning up in the atmosphere, leaving everyone gasping –

Working Debenhams' Late Shift
Sheffield floods, November 7th 2019

If this is a preview of the end of the world,
my phone is a reel of red alerts and head office
still don't want us to go home. They say things like,
we can't tell until it happens and then all the buses
are cancelled. I count eight raindrops per second
from the single stamp window in the stockroom
by the clicked parcels that won't be collected.
An umbrella shouts up, *it's a hell of a night*
and I believe it, walking faster as I set off under
what once were streetlamps – now unidentified
flickering objects. Dad texts, *I'm coming through town,
where are you*. I say, *I've passed the pyjama-striped
cinema, am stood by the undressed trees and manikins,
it's cold* and then I spot his bald head like the dome
of a temple. Like the splashed shine of a boar snout
polished bronze in Florence. If you rubbed it,
it promised your return. *We'll have toast
when we get home*, he says as we slip into step
and a silence thick and buttery. A student takes
her bicycle for a walk, then a swim. A wrung dishcloth
of a spaniel is carried. A tent floats upside down.
Nice weather for ducks, a man calls and laughs
like a thunderclap. All I know is my dad rolls up
his trouser legs, wades knee-high into the underpass
which thrums like the dark centre of my gran's
macular degeneration where straight lines run crooked
and there are only eddies of the peripheral.
And I worry I am missing what's important.
Yet he hums, *can't go over it, can't go under it …*
and when the asteroid strikes, when the locusts plague,

when the angels come down with minted rage
and inexorable glory I know they'll have to stay
their blazing hands for the father who waits
for his daughter while she empties out her boots.

Acknowledgements

A huge thank you firstly needs to go to my family, especially my parents, for always supporting my writing, even when I was teeny-tiny and comparing clouds to fluffy sheep. Thank you to both of you, and especially my mum, for wading through far too many first drafts and always honestly saying what she thought. I do not think I would have kept writing without you!

To all the incredible friends in my life, and my partner – I love you all and am always thankful for your belief in me. Thank you for putting up with me during my busiest times and still being there when I return!

I am massively indebted to various writing communities who have given me the self-confidence necessary to put myself out there in the world as a poet. Hive Young Writers and, most importantly, Vicky Morris, have been integral to that, as have my UEA MA tutors Tiffany Atkinson, Sophie Robinson and Andrea Holland. An important shout-out also goes to the Ilkley Literature Festival for believing in my writing since I was a child and still as an adult – those small, early poetry successes in competitions meant everything to me.

I'm grateful to Kim Moore for liking these poems enough to select them and offering me her invaluable mentorship, as well as Vanessa Lampert and Katrina Naomi for writing such lovely back cover reviews for me – I can only hope to be deserving of those wonderful recommendations from poets I admire so much. Likewise, The Poetry Business and Peter Sansom, who have made this entire process possible.

Lastly, but no less importantly, a thank you to each of the following competitions and publications who have selected or printed these poems: *After Hours* (Hive South Yorkshire); *Beaver Magazine*; *Bi+ Lines: An Anthology of Contemporary Bi+ Poets* (Fourteen Poems); *Black Nore Review*; Bridport Poetry Prize; Ginkgo Prize; Ilkley Literature Festival; Ink, Sweat and Tears; Mslexia Poetry Competition; The National Poetry Competition; *The Poetry Review*; UEA MA Anthology and Winchester Poetry Prize. I was delighted to be chosen by you and included in your publications.